ANTHOLOGY ATRIUMS

ANTHOLOGY ATRIUMS

Anthony P Prior

atmosphere press

© 2024 Anthony P Prior

Published by Atmosphere Press

Cover design by Ronaldo Alves
Cover image by Anthony P Prior

No part of this book may be reproduced without permission from the author except in brief quotations and in reviews.

Atmospherepress.com

CONTENTS

SHORT ANGRY

Telephone cut off can only report by mobile,
Nobody there so leave message appealing for
help,
Internet is also marginal.
Dependency is highlighted in need,
Independent don't like relying on others,
Must control temper my temper,
Occupying myself writing about dichotomy,
Time ticks on waiting not relating,
Distant have got no resistance,
Don't know who to call on if I could.
Trepidation poor relation confiscation,
Taken away my play serious furious,
Now making a meal of bad deal,
Can't conceal how I feal unreal,
A technical problem left me in doldrums,
My conundrum all at sea drowning.

WONDERFUL WARWICKSHIRE

My home county born and raised here,
I have travelled and lived away but always
returned home to wonderful
Warwickshire,
It's a flat county with small undulations,
Steep hills to cycle up down over across,
Neatly cut hedge rows trees abut with gates,
Copses interspaced marking out ley lines,
Churches mark out villages from history,
Ordnance survey maps adjoin hitherto,
Guy Fawkes plotted in my village Dunchurch,
Lord Catesby main plotter Catesby House,
Wealth featured by grandiose presence,
Long straight roads linked by hedges,
The Fosse Way cuts straight through it,
Castles feature Shakespeare acts in Stratford,
Weally Wonderful Warwickshire.

BUILDINGSOUL

We need architecture to represent us,
To work ergonomically for us,
In harmony knowing complimenting,
A natural flow shortcut easy,
Space to move not claustrophobic,
Open space respectful reflection,
Not hidden dangerous concealed,
Promoting pleasing revealing,
Artistic sculptures harmonising grace,
Fashionable fashioned loosely,
Welcoming open arms,
Disabled friendly all-inclusive,
Graffiti wall for expression,
Skateboard park areas,
All-weather seating lounges,
Unthretening walkways,
Lean-to cycle bays,
No traffic slow pace.

LAYMAN'S ALGORITHM

Listening to the radio about DNA potential,
How it's charged and made up,
Not just double helix found by Crick and Watson,
But further mathematical equations breaking down,
Building blocks of its structure algorithms that have,
Potential to grow and change develop into,
A different structure more complex diverse,
Analysing building blocks finding cures for,
Diseases cancers where DNA has grown,
Incorrectly the genome structure grown,
Wrongly not offering strength where needed,
Cancers developed overactive displaced,
Grown in haste progressive directive,
Overgrowing messages wrong number,
Answered rudely not wanted stubborn,
Salesman won't go away here to play,
Take an advance unnatural sequence,
Causing deliverance overgrown place,
Destroy only way to correct directly,
Or disobey comes into play,
Balance correct substance perchance,
Shrivel away unwanted growth by chemistry.

CHECKMATE

Got to adhere to strict rules of taking

medication as a drug test to be able to

continue taking the aforesaid,

Not happy with this they insist,

A statutory requirement for my sake,

Talked into this by professionals,

I say I'll comply and won't defy,

I feel like a crash test dummy,

My pleasing nature abused,

Because I know the nature,

Of this is scientific research,

Proven disposition complies.

REVEAL HOW I FEEL

A day older from retirement,
This is no big deal, same old spiel,
Nothing changed just mind rearranged,
With ideas of freedom, can do anything,
The choice is don't look back,
Positive forward, don't like change keep plain,
Simplistic realistic a head thing thinks straight,
Stick to what I know above below don't you,
Life leads the way in all decency,
Boring but proven common sense,
Ordinary sets a pattern proven,
Age gives assured authority,
In all decency be decent,
Conscience clears no fear,
Confident confidential,
Expressing orderly order,
Representing presence of mind,
Fun be kind all the same remind,
Project projecting acceptance,
With my kind of difference.

ALL ABOUT SPACE

Got plenty should really narrow down,
Move to smaller house makes sense,
Throw out paraphernalia junk,
Rearrange layout.
Make areas more efficient,
I have ideas visualise change,
Make do with what I've got,
Balance out not used,
Bring back into use disused,
Things have got their place,
Well remembered common place,
Don't like change anyway,
Ergonomic best way this way,
Transfer transcribe efficiency,
Keep the same rearrange,
Adjust everything has its place,
Tried and tested homely at home,
Don't condone new platform,
Same but different relent,
Pull-out clean around,
This seems new arbitrary can-do.

NEGLECT DEFECTS

From prospective clientele who might,
Be able to confront problems encountered,
When undertaking difficult jobs needing,
Experienced advice with building problems,
A correction of faulty work needing attention,
Forthwith to redress the said encumbrance,
This should be carried out as soon as possible,
To rectify further damage to unstable wall,
About to fall due to bad workmanship,
Damage at this stage could be unsurmountable,
In cost if not stopped "stich in time saves nine,"
Making the afore imperative to correct,
Without panicking or burying head in sand,
The job has landed me in deep water,
From which I ought to bail out pout!
I get in touch with builder friend about,
"Mend" his advice is sound I concur,
Not to defer or pretend any longer,
Minds combine to solve resolve,
Defect warrants imperative directive,
To set straight no later than late.

A JOURNEY

First, I must get my trike repaired,
New wheel bearings fitted by engineer,
Must commandeer suitable one,
Yes, got it sorted now away for the day,
Set off down the back road,
Luckily, most of Warwickshire,
Where I live is flat cycling country,
Few hills or steep inclines,
It's popular cycling with wide clear roads,
Pelotons of cyclist's frequent routes,
It's no main carriage or highway,
To anywhere apart from farms,
Singular houses isolated villages,
With pub a stop off drink and grub,
Well oiled setting off again the aim,
Is to circumnavigate a round trip,
From home and back avoiding busy,
Main roads cars that goads patience,
That I lose with them, they bully,
And dangerously force ways through,
Cars rule fools out of my way,
Don't cause delay.

FUN-FOR-ALL

Joyce's sad occasion a funeral,
Shock at Bob's demise,
Meeting up with old friends,
Haven't seen for years,
Identifying seeing through wear and tear,
How it's changed all of us,
Still the same old characters,
Changed rearranged,
Faces drawn eyes bright,
Diminished stance,
Essence humoured humorously,
Joyous convivially,
Commiserations collective,
Harmonious directive,
Friends all the same,
Courage drink and be merry.

PARTS OF LIFE

I don't like, I could name them all,
Be a bore I'm sure you'll agree,
Obvious life's expectancy,
I expect too much,
Being disabled limited enabled,
Like to be in control of destiny,
My destiny controls me,
There seems to be a conformity,
Morally obliged obligation,
Adhere to expected expectancy,
Ways mapped out certainly,
Certain certificate duration,
Time allotted apportioned,
Dereliction of duties derelict,
Conscious conscience conscious,
Inflammatory inflammation flared.

SOMETHING
IN THE AIR EITHER

A lot happening dynamically,
Football police being called,
Aggressive behaviour restrictions flouted,
Bashing noises crashing shouting,
Breaking entering demands,
All happening tonight,
Get on it names taken,
Official presence restricts,
Regional accents present bother,
No apparent reasons uncovered,
Frustrations gained momentum,
Pally ally crass ass play up,
Testosterone fuelled aggression,
Jesting for a fight tonight,
Relationships split apart,
Come to a head dread,
Fear at rear appear,
Consultations restricted,
Reported to appropriate services,
Health and safety matey,
Avoiding calamity.

ACHIEVED SOMETHING

———

Bought a new pair of trainers,

Specifically for walking on my treadmill,

They seem a good fit need wearing in,

Got to take shape of my foot,

Keep them on all day get used to,

The treadmill is new as well,

A novel approach to improve walking,

Not just talking about it doing,

Improving my balance this chance,

The trainers seem good but I,

Realise walking coordination,

Is vital to purposefully striding out,

Maintaining a rhythm important,

On the treadmill to keep it going,

Not stopping trying to recover,

From a standing start is an art,

Practice is going to help improve,

Getting in the groove loosely truly,

So I can achieve believe,

In my ability to proceed surely.

EXPONENTIAL

An increasing number progression,
Of space expanding performance,
Enlarging getting deeper theatrical,
Mathematical equation adding up bigger,
Equates to more space beyond further out,
Equation representing enlargement more,
Adds up to not finished yet done or final,
Original has been outdated updated,
Going on and on about its boring deliberation,
Congregating crowds full don't let any more in,
Bit of a squeeze hot getting hotter boiling,
Push comes to shove falling over wild rover,
Bought a bargain now a pretty penny heavenly,
Investments grow kept at large larger bumper,
Unit price doubled sold quadrupled over and over,
Growth growing consoling consumption consumer,
Alphabet pegboard abacus clocking up counting,
Money lenders lending collateral spending,
Banks banking save spend mortgage borrow,
Infinite number infinity Infiniti no end constant.

MY IMAGINATION

Is extensive expressive no boundaries or limits,
Fun humour entice,
All things lovely, nice,
Play at charm charming,
Doing no harm just warming up,
Joking evoking a laugh,
Joining in a gaff,
Testing how far to go,
Push and retrieve believe,
All-inclusive humours,
Boundaries tested,
Crude not molested,
Not too far door ajar,
Let in quips and whips,
Pleasure tips ups downs,
Clown's frowns smile trial,
Denials compiled.
Lame game portrayed,
Pulling your leg,
Beg borrow steal,
Enough for a meal,
Drink and be merry cheers.

NOT PROVEN

Something from imagination imagined pretend,
Innocent until proven guilty of said occurrences,
Weight is put on the defender to dispel,
Caught out defence offered against administration,
Incurred deferred procrastination put-off rebuffed,
Rehabilitation offered against dissimulation with,
No correlation or attribution against pretence,
Common sense doesn't figure disfigured,
Admission of guilt characterful caricature,
Lies tried and tested manifested prophetic,
I'll admit I shouldn't have don't chastise my,
Demise when I'm surprised as you are that,
Evidence put forward doesn't suit my recompense,
Diligence deferred later to contemplate,
Commiserate complicates all delegates,
Adhered to a decision abruptly dysfunctionally,
Incurs abbreviated abbreviations forthwith,
Or without further raconteur beautiful demure.
Absolute absolution absolute authority.
You can't be serious me lord.

REMISSION

From the dreaded C no more treatment,
Fantastic news I feel light on my feet,
Unburdened my burden, set myself free,
All a bit heady, unusual new bit casual,
Have left shock behind don't remind,
How dreadful it's been innocent me,
Didn't fully understand my calamity,
Or fully believe what could happen,
It was caught early treated immediately,
Chemotherapy tablets on trial might work,
No choice, bring it on, responding,
Sick feeling must be working,
Under supervision monitored,
Drips administered antibiotics,
Seemed to be doing well as far as I could tell,
Side effects didn't have much hair to lose,
Be brave take it on the chin begin again,
Nearly lost everything life becoming,
Life's worth resolutely resolved,
Know it all won't be told know how,
Put in to question how it all began,
Soul searching finding soul.

ABOUT TIME

Things are expected to come about,
As a matter of order routine,
Expected delivery on time,
Setup executed each semester,
Taken care of not short,
Order of play no delay,
Time ordered manner,
Direct debit account,
Gets paid automatically,
Less virtual contact the better,
Don't bother sending letter,
No pitter-patter,
On time reminds,
Function functionality,
Punctual delivery,
Late delegates,
Library ticket expires,
Return items,
Back cash back
Cash in,
Insolvent returns,
Accountant alarmed.

SOLVING PROBLEMS

That's life get to work make things easier,
Start analysing what's important.
Don't want to let my disability be,
A hindrance to myself and others,
I am driven to achieve,
Always must be busy and am,
Challenged by issues arising,
Solutions solved resolved,
Hitch straightened out,
Use my clout,
Leave nothing out,
Derisions sing,
Loud and clear,
Comprise of smear,
Oh dear I fear,
Slang prang,
Have done wrong,
Correcting all along,
Make better to the letter,
Words hold key,
Play on song,
Sing it applaud it.

LOOKING

I'm looking for something but don't know what it's
called,
There must be a file on the computer with it on,
You must be so specific to narrow it down,
Now feel lost in the maelstrom of possibilities,
I must give up looking get on doing,
Start afresh it will be better this time,
With a different state of mind,
I have a picture to combine,
Words in a song ear wormed drive,
Me along the song I sing along in my head,
The tune backing harmoniously in time,
Jovial combine gets my job done easily,
Now come to think of it I'll look elsewhere,
What comes to mind is a date and time,
What else I was doing sure going to find,
My predicament is out time I'm left behind,
Now want to catch up newfound reason to,
Push on take and make forsaken mistaken,
Advances that don't enhance my chances,
Of viewing perchance looking forward onward.

ALL FOR NOTHING

Sometimes it seems like it's a lot of bother,
Trying hard with little reward, must try harder,
Sometimes you must change tack for less flak,
Try a different route way of finding your way,
A different approach makes more sense to,
Change now before too late compensate literally,
I hate to deliberate profusely rather than loosely,
But conductively orchestrate harmony,
Sounds in tune with what I'm looking for,
I've done before and want some more,
Finding a new way with difficulty,
Many times, changed my routine,
To alleviate glean combat obscene,
Without a visit to the latrine having been,
Didn't make it on time the look on my face,
My wife says "Change of pants dear!"
Intuitive women always right taking the piss,
MS has weakened my resolve to hold,
Embarrassment harassment relief belief,
"Good grief!" Not again complain strain,
When I go out, I must wear a convene,
Piped to a leg bag to conceal relieved,

ADAPTING REALISING

Keeping up with modern life is strife,
I know what's going on but don't understand,
Everything has got complicated a bit tricky,
Responsibilities implicated strangle me,
All the time there seem to be new problems,
Created implicated demands reprimands,
Bills presented orders ordered can't afford,
Must not ignore deplore carry on absorbed,
Got better things to do leave me alone condone,
Now got sucked in as a sucker.
Won't stand for that foolish prat,
Wanting more don't care for greed,
Officious duplicitous derogatory,
Condescending putdown frown,
Realistically realising unadapting,
Lost out no doubt oblivious now,
Can't adapt to what I don't understand,
Not what I planned adapting making a stand,
It comes as a shock but shouldn't be mocked.

WATCHING BUT NOT WATCHING

Time to put the telly on, get the news,
Taking it all in nothing new after listening to radio,
Bad news is good news sensational views,
Paramount importance is top of agenda,
Shocking can't look away has me held,
Now I've got the daily dirt numb hurt,
Something lighter polite drama unfolds,
Seen before knowing what's going to happen,
Drift into character association,
Acting play drama theatrical way,
All the expected same acted out,
Watching but not watching similar scenes,
Seen it happen before wanting more,
Documentaries demand more attention,
Following misrepresentation unfold,
All told presence annulled when bold,
Drawn in plot thickens schemes redeems,
Solved evolved solutions repelled,
Purposefully been told consoled,
Future changed must rearrange,

Lost the plot doesn't matter anyway,
Anyone can play same old tune buffoon,
Midnight noon awake from slumber,
Mid-summer-night-dreamer.*
*Thanks, Shaky!

SIFT THROUGH

Having to wade through Monday's dross,

Before I can get started get real I feel,

Confidence tricksters tricking confidently,

Got personal details done homework,

As if I'm a jerk nonsense convince,

Plausible benefit those on benefits,

Small fee to comply can't deny,

Phone number to activate as of late,

Accommodate or confiscate up to date,

Hasn't gained mine so I decline to play,

Foolish fool what do you take me for?

Capitulate navigate away from dodgy scene,

Won't let it come in between being obscene,

Know what I mean last to see controversy,

Naive taken in sod off harassing don't touch it,

Conflict got basic simply simplistic now awake,

It's a jungle out there innocent warfare.

VIEW ALL AROUND

———

My front door faces north and opens out into a,
Porch so I open and shut quickly to keep out chilly,
Winds at bay difficult when I have a caller,
Ringing front doorbell then entertain them,
In the porch, sometimes a party atmosphere,
Develops with friends calling in the private,
Contained space the rat-race on the street outside.
Abide with hide and chat falling back on memories,
Remember that laugh split sides confides with
happenings,
Way back then if only we could live like that now,
Happy days full of praise no delays foot down,
Full steam ahead going for it up a winding country
lane,
Hand built stone walls sheep and cattle in fields
behind,
Serves to remind me of old times when we first met,
My partner from a whole new colloquial northern
accent,
Which I was to frequent I was shown novelty dives,

Down old town lanes and told of stories of,

Student frequents and how they lived,

Introduced to some of those haunts and,

27

WALKING CLINIC

———

Had a video taken of me walking,
Now back on my good medication,
The result was fairly good,
My stride was smoother,
Lifting my knee and leg,
A set distance four times,
Maintained a rhythm,
Turned kept going,
Balance steady,
Saw myself looking good,
Not stumbling,
Confidently reflecting,
This was done for UCLH,
Preview telephone appointment,
I think I passed test,
Better on medication,
Than off for their trial,
Proven rigmarole,
Test proves best,
Usual conquest.

SLIPPING AWAY

———

Can't believe I'm lost for words that sick,

Don't know what to do, looking around,

Sample over ripe plums spit it out stone fluid,

Tasteless useless real mess nonetheless,

Demands wash hands wipe floor,

Sun is burning through consider rude,

Do anything I don't really want to and do,

Simply simple commiserations doable,

Derive the contrive considerable considered,

Deferred differences obscured obsolete,

Obsessions get a hold and won't let go,

Each to their own I don't condone,

Prone to ridicule the unfortunates,

It could happen to anybody and does,

Simply sympathise with not so privileged,

Forthwith or without loss of foothold,

Slipping away timeless sympathy,

Needed to dispel same old controversy,

Of time ordered irregularities regularly,

A slip of a girl slips her slips on slips away.

VISION

Different wavelengths project different colours,
Nocturnal not so good at night photo receptors,
We have better colour reception than other
animals, making us dominant
species,
Pick up different wavelengths compared,
Dogs' vision isn't as good as ours but make up,
For it with more sensitive hearing picking up,
On a wide range of noises higher and lower,
Pitches, receptors acknowledge differences,
Which is why dogs are good companions,
Protecters defenders of territory terribly,
We use colour to identify objects ripe ready,
Ultra-violet light is seen more by insects,
Light from the sun is picked up in many ranges,
Detected reflected shadows bright night light,
Eyes adapt focus clearly brilliantly receptive.

PRETTY FAIR

To be fair I dare to be different,
Fair enough I hear you say in all commonalities,
It's only fair for those who dare with functionality,
With good reason pleasing purposefully,
With my electric eye set to defy don't pry,
Difference is differential noncommittal,
Fairly presumptuous prominently,
Environmentally consequential discriminately,
Delivering fare does to lunch time fare,
Sold at the country fair fairly regularly,
Frequently frequenting similar disbursements,
Disturbing regular fair play fairly conventional,
Discriminating fair regulations fluctuating unfairly,
Unbalanced fair play inconsiderate deficiency,
Alleviating discrepancies with tendencies to,
Tell lies far too often regular fairly,
Indiscriminately discriminating far-off places,
Not in touch with reality not being fair to be fair.

SETTING THE CLOCK

Read the instructions,

Time is arbitrary personal,

The mean standard is set,

By an atomic clock Greenwich

Meantime, in London,

This is the standard start,

For every clock worldwide,

There are time zones for all other countries,

Due to position on the planet,

The magnetic field of Earth affects,

Compasses magnetic fields,

Starting from Greenwich,

Magnetic north set for all maps,

This standard has been set for all,

Then calibrated moving away from start.

I feel privileged to be at the centre,

Belonging to Newton's Laws,

An English professor,

Has set the standard for all to follow.

DING-DING-DING

A reminder not to forget pay attention,
Repeating in case I forget obnoxiously,
Ok! I get it ringing in my ear for fear,
Ordered to act on robotic notion,
Computerized command repetitive demand,
Act now or get below standards set,
Not emotional personal referral,
Again, pertain positive complain,
Persistent jurisdiction completion,
Final retort not to abort caught,
Demanded reprimanded commanded,
For the best don't contest play along,
Obliged confided assertive provided,
Getting with it compulsive deficit,
Distractions delude true aims,
Complain drains what remains,
Must satisfy rhythmic alibi,
Made a lot of noise over nothing,
Consolatory singing ding-a-ling.

PEACE OF MIND

It's important to know yourself,
Your limits, interests, preferred ways,
Distractions can impose without realizing,
They have a way of demanding attention,
Don't get taken in as gullible sucker,
Trickery seems part of the game,
Devious plausible only trust reliable,
Careful of over-friendly approach,
Scheming troublemaker's fakers,
Most people are decent friendly,
What you expect as you would do yourself,
It comes down to who you can trust,
Friend or foe, detect directly effect,
When you're happy tentatively proceed,
Have a business mind share kind,
Build trust is a must engage don't lose faith,
Normal ways are set up to follow,
Fair enough stuff common decency,
Reason reasonably peacefully.

KEEP WARM

Cold snap chilled me to the core,

Couldn't warm up chilly Parky,

Bit slow irritable put on thermals,

Felt more together not in the altogether,

Change whatever the weather,

Reacting adapting from within,

Common sense sinking in,

Practical thoughts adding up,

Look after yourself good health,

Don't abuse get confused,

Call a truce on setting loose,

Warm within when cold out,

Cold will make you feel old,

Move about food for energy,

When life is as boring as hell,

Concentrate on keeping well,

Warm heart keeps a part of,

Friendly conversations good relations.

AFFECTED BY

Can't help being affected by "news" on the radio,
Bad news is good news to sellers of said,
Don't like what people can do to each other sister,
Brother lover another bet rover condoner,
Life's a risky biscuit dunk ability poor,
Over-saturated with enforced deplore law,
What for? Can't ignore assertive directive,
When it's common practice in place race,
Disagreeable disagreeing again and again,
Doesn't fit in my picture frame get the picture?
Must retain decent decency commonality,
People's different ways display differences,
Phrases abusive not conclusive affection,
Wrong or right contrite power-plays blowup,
Continue to assert alert disturbed perverts,
Continued apprehension reprehensible,
Defenceless defence able incorrigible,
Directly affected inscrutable effects,
Florescent on their continued continuum,
Shining a light on their plight assertively.

LOTS TO DO

Busy time of the year,
Christmas year-end presents of mind,
Planning thinking ahead of jobs at hand,
Annoying holdups stop the flow undertow,
Stopping progression adapt recollect,
Overcoming conundrum has left me in doldrums,
Chancing ideas come into my head mostly mad,
Thought it abandon get real how I feel,
Excitement doesn't fit too early feeling yearly,
Scatterbrain remains in charge criminal at large,
Anything could happen lost all recollection,
Thinking my way through jumping on true,
Certify clarifies rectify mistakes made better,
To the letter precisely perfectionist contest,
Making work for myself not settling for less,
Not happy with averaging out little spittle,
Acquitted acquittal acquisitions acquired.
Nonetheless empty vessel sinking,
Plenty of noise sinking feeling know what,
I'm meaning contravening said and done.

ACTIVE

Ok, always active from the start simple motion,
My routine kicks in then I'm away,
Sorting out problems ordering order,
Controlling realising intruders asking,
Too many questions persistent provocateurs,
Deviant deviators grabbers grabbing groping,
Looking for any way in picking up on something I,
Said, sharp criminal sounding gullible me,
Noncommittal not trivial, hang up call back,
Not taking no for an answer I defer to say,
Won't go away stalking no decency,
This soft thieving action discriminatory,
Wanting details to derail order prevail,
Learnt not to give in to bullying condescending,
Silly boys trying to get away with improper,
Morality sounding stupidly confident realistic,
Not going to fall for idiotic presented drama,
Write me a letter for me to consider considerate,
They've gone away but hacked into details,
Private dysfunctionality criminally confidentiality.

PUT ON

First you put on get dressed,
I'm now presentable to go out,
Early morning swim take off said,
Sixteen lengths shower,
Put back on warm attire,
Fashionable for shopping,
Try on new wears,
Off with old put on new,
Wear home comfortable,
Worn and trod in wearable,
New wears I dare,
Good fit I like it,
Reflection carried,
Borrowed married,
Put on together,
Wherewithal,
Confident front,
Brave face put on,
Suits my equation.
A put on.

KEEPING HOPEFUL

Yes, got to don't want to bring others down,
Everything you do reflects effects,
On the line better refine time,
Do it for myself contribution health,
Confidence shows don't stoop below,
Not always easy to be strong believe me,
Accepting normally receive reflect direct,
Trying my best with life's conquest,
Dealt with ordinary boring talking reasoning,
Mood is light kept alright bright,
Conversation comply ideas reply,
Contribution offering solution,
Shared solved resolved,
Left alone dissolved,
Problems sort themselves,
Happy to allow here and now,
Considerate concessions,
Bearing true reflections.
Hopeful determinations.

KNOW YOUR LIMITS

Sometimes I get in a self-imposed confused state,

In the thick of it struggle to get out of it,

Walk away can be easier said than done,

My tricky conundrum tripping over wild rover,

Only to discover needn't have bothered,

Made a problem out of nothing trying too hard,

It's difficult to leave alone problems moan,

Thought I was doing the right thing resolving,

Tied the knot tighter tripping over bound over,

Trying to keep the peace no release sorry tale,

Fought tooth and nail problem still prevails,

Derails my don't-turn-to-easy-solution confidence,

Taken away drink debauchery never say never,

Think clever! Leave alone unrefined twisted minds,

Who want to unfairly lay bare as if you don't care,

Promiscuous derogatory insolent solutions,

Forthwith without due consideration of misfortune,

Be posted on hitherto's conundrum unfairly.

YULE TIME

A pagan log celebrating Christmas special time,
Celebrating the winter solstice giving thanks,
A ritual remembering Christianity blessing,
The end of the year bringing on the new,
Festive singing and dancing eating drinking,
Celebrating offering gifts sharing partaking,
Remembered every year giving and taking,
Dining with traditional turkey excessively,
Fine wines ports spices mince pies cake,
Plentiful renewal giveth taketh maketh,
Drink and be merry celebration partying,
Thinking of sending cards remembering,
Exchanging offering taking returning,
Yule log yearning contributing befriending,
Friends remembered contributing,
Gathering solidarity proving improving.

KNOW YOURSELF

Makes advances easier,
Not wasting time on trivia,
Trivial pursuits costs loots,
Ideas in my head must be said,
Precious confidence diligence,
Abide by usual ways displays,
Kept in turn literal spurns,
Comeback referred deferred,
Know my place in the race,
No disgrace loss of face,
Similar dissimilar familiar,
Fortune favours the brave,
Boldly into next masquerade,
Pretentious or presumptuous,
Prevalent keen as mustard,
Keeping on toes only knows,
Disposed left behind remind,
Positive advance known,
Sure thing confidence sings.

ACCEPTING CHANGE

Different rearrange of ideas plans,
The same but different order of order,
Made interesting by persisting,
Belligerent listing consisting resisting,
Benefiting nobody shoddy job,
Not good for anybody unruly,
Behaviour expecting too much,
Of such and such ditch authority,
Plainly proceed do what you need,
Logically work through what to do,
Symbiotic relationships can symbolise,
Change is needed to influence progress,
Good progression different direction,
Opportunities open up fresh appeal,
Attractive positive directive taken,
If I'm not mistaken good solution,
Incentive is more money the driver,
Profit from consideration definite,
Solution making a gain rearrange.

GEORGE MICHAEL

A natural flamboyant singer star,
Complete confident personality,
Vivacious upfront performer,
Dynamic strong voice,
Defining greatness oneness,
Soul singer soul man,
Bearing his soul expressing,
Life's struggle revealed,
Nothing concealed,
Theatrical performer,
Strategic strategy,
Full of hope,
Underneath sadness shows,
Brave front covers up,
Live performance reveals,
Tender tendencies,
Ever longing for recognition,
Singing emotionally,
Really, he's crying,
A lost soul trying.

TRUST IN OTHERS

That's a bit scary when you have got a paranoid mind,
Have been let down previously,
I should trust people more but reticent,
I usually do with a guard, defence held,
Open with friendly meld upheld,
Enjoy people's company a lot to me,
My reserved inventory deliberately,
Humour breaks the ice barriers down,
Humoured humours draw together,
Curtains keep warm cold out,
Well insulated not related,
Poor impoverished defenceless,
Sleep on the street wrapped up,
Walk on by example to defy,
To us all societies refuge,
Don't have to live like one,
Refugee helpless commodity,
Implausible to upper classes,
Held in trust always must repost.

KEEPING IN TOUCH

It's too easy to get removed from friends and
family end of year,
I can get detached from people not bothering,
New year's resolution to communicate better,
Keep in touch with people I know,
I have been thinking it's not important wrong,
It's easy so do remember to do,
Didn't think I was important enough to comment,
So, I braved it and joined the clan be a man,
Social media is there, decided to care,
Put in an opinion and stood back,
I can stand making a stand any reprimand.
Hope to hear back from those I know,
Don't want to be disposed of,
Keeping in step conforming,
Friends knowing make amends,
Good reliable couldn't do without all,
Simple easy to do reprimand stiff stand,
Lost command of senses representing,
Myself drink to good health!

CALCULATED RISKS

Of course, too much caution knows what's going,
The unpredictable can always happen it does,
Prepare for the worst overdressed does,
Confide be on the safe side,
Taken the fun out of living not so forgiving,
Exciting risk-taking contemplating chancing,
Go-for-it bravado something new seeing true,
Taken in trust must comply surely will,
Comforting to know natural course of course,
Risks don't need to be taken get mistaken,
For a fool dribbling old mule stabled unable,
Think of end goal gather draw in calculating,
Life's mission is to achieve have faith believe,
Confidence in ability shows no risk at all,
When likely to fall risk taken forsaken,
Oblivious symptomatic symptoms sympathise,
Derisory confiders provide no gain only complain,
Calculated prodigiously faith in harmony.

NEW YEAR, 2024

Brand new just the same but different,
In the way of atmosphere feeling,
Made a resolution friendly talking,
Not too abrupt seeing differences,
Others' point of view understanding,
Change of ways different displays,
Don't want to interfere make clear,
Space freedom room to move,
Still routine orders play for the day,
Quiet opening easy happening,
Approached the same different display,
Newness has a smoothness.
Thinking ahead what can I do,
Within my means what I mean,
Sensible practical practice,
Listening hearing acting,
Defer playacting get real,
Responsibly respond forthwith.

AI SETTINGS

Can be good making light of ordinary work,
A good program orders and delivers set results,
Professional unquestionable standard delivered,
Official office documenting delivering certainty,
Confidential conscience considered correctly,
Having confidence in progressive development,
Moral consideration correctly considered,
Not forgotten or left out program planned,
Set straight encountering encounters,
Equivocally correctly all said and done,
Confidence gained pertained posthumously,
Rigorously tried and tested all collected,
Functional deliberate considerate,
Consideration fitting into planned plans,
Artificial intelligence delivering recommends,
Pretentious configuration regulates script,
Second to nondigital format configures,
Explicit direction deliberately obscured.

REPETITIVE REPEAT

A lot of things have to be confirmed as done,
It's always best to check for yourself,
For any mistakes omissions incorrect,
Or maybe it's meant to be deliberately,
Writings metre rap singing over again,
Words rhyme rhythm repetitive chime,
Songs repeat verses over and over,
Doing the same thing singing makes easier,
Boring repetitive sings along strong,
Jovial hearty sings true a can-do,
Tapping rapping drumming forthcoming,
Symbols syllables trivial tantalised,
All said and done isn't 'til it's done,
Metal worker taps rhythm to beat,
Finish finishing off annealed revealed,
Punishing replenished harnessing,
Television repeats remind time gone by,
Will watch again and again renew frame,
Know where we are repetitive positive,
Seen it before will watch some more,
What a bore.

SAID GOOD NIGHT

But it wasn't I was reliving all my problems,
Mashed them fought through solved,
Anger management got involved controlled,
Answered relived never again refrain,
Pulled all the covers won victory all mine,
Battles in my head fraught caught out,
Woke grumpy fatherless contest,
Couldn't lie in with confrontation,
Sprang out of bed ditch said,
Dreams had evolved into formidable,
Scary monsters shrugged them off,
Given all-clear by sunny morning,
New day dawning refreshed still alive,
Back of my mind don't need to remind,
Get on with something anything convalescing,
All so much clearer clearly dearly,
For fear of nearly losing the plot,
Imagination poor relation configuration,
Disturbed confrontation solved.

PICTURE THIS

Daguerreotype first photographs 1839,

Exposed on silver plate,

Victorian image capturing a moment in time,

Negative image printed as positive effect,

Taking the spirit of life in an instant,

Now modern-day digital pixilated images,

Capture this fragment needing no chemicals,

To develop and print a pixel format picture,

Good camera lenses have been developed,

By N.A.S.A. space technology for our use,

Through mobile phones digital cameras,

Technology offering a full range,

In focus near and far portrait landscape,

A holistic approach imaging formatting,

Filming videoing security cameras noting,

Reporting newspapers internet documenting,

The digital world assessing everything,

Taking note bespoke details reveals,

All encompassed visualised reported.

RETIREMENT

Funny to think I've reached that age, but I have,
Feel young at heart now pensioner,
Always wondered what an O.A.P. was,
Qualifying for benefits discounts,
At the hairdressers cheap entry,
A whole new ball game of done time,
Paid my debts to society, into the big pot,
Time to take it easy, how horrible no way,
Give us a job, want to feel useful can do,
Sit back and relax armchair parasite,
A delinquent irresponsibly responsible,
I want to have fun on the run diddle-dum,
Don't want to be retarded retired,
Preferential treatment referred resolutely,
Complicated competitor competing,
Never say die knocking on the door.

TAKES AWAY

I enjoy writing a cathartic method of,
Communicating expressing feelings,
About topical and memories experiences,
Thinking and engaging reporting lyrically,
Writing helps me question reevaluate,
Directing good sense of order directly,
This method laid out orderly and correct,
Has right effect assembled dialect.
Understood open intriguing believing,
All this knowledge experience given away,
I'm happy to offer this opportunity gain,
An altruistic beneficial benefit all for,
Personally, very satisfying pleasing,
To give not always take grown up,
Share compare condition fair,
It doesn't take away good nature,
I'm resembling forth giving away.

HAND TO MOUTH

A lot of life is still very basic, functional,
Having to live within our means,
No matter how wealthy or well-to-do,
Cash flow governs our remittance,
Of what we allow ourselves to spend,
Still a balancing act in out about,
Nothing much to it construe it,
Revolve around trapped compound,
Freedom let me out lots to shout about,
Limitations poor relations considerable,
Considerations add up to dysfunctional,
Arbitrary communications forthwith,
Without relinquishing hitherto forth,
That cometh from within differentiating,
Conundrum residing in conscious,
Conscience hidden from obvious,
Oblivious obstructions pending,
Immediate arbitration to reset,
The balance of aforesaid continuum.

THINGS OUTSTANDING

A level of importance orders my order,
What can wait I'll delegate leave out,
Omissions placed on the back burner,
They will probably always catch a catch,
This foreseen want to leave behind,
Until I get a reminder bill to be paid,
Of course, I'll pay, usual month delay,
Credit where credit's due off to Timbuktu,
I must remember before I leave to read,
Road maps set sat nav to find way back,
Way back then continued conundrum,
Silly rude misconstrued conciliatory,
Consolation contributing to deformation,
Avoiding irregular regulations regularly,
But I can't keep putting it off won't do,
Want to get up to date as of late considerate,
Jobs commanding preference due diligence,
Given half the chance put off procrastinate,
Outstanding not too demanding deviations.

PLACE POSITIONING

First start by reckoning where you want to be,
Not easy without repeating, same but different,
New angle, realign objectives to suit,
I want to achieve something new fresh,
I'm always me all comes from my compatibility,
Ideas in my head project way to connect,
Must get ahead to keep creative momentum,
Rolling along, thoughts of something new,
Old but adapted to fit in with this feeling stance,
Approached in different way, mood colours,
Represent different outlook to my advance,
Take a chance prepare with flair au-contraire,
Now must dig deep to bring about change,
Not really change just rearrange placing,
Space affecting each other juxtaposition,
Changes the dynamics relationship,
This is offering me a new representation,
An affiliation of place positioning forthwith.

GOOD CRAIC

I went on a trip to Ireland and the craic was good,

A good atmosphere of fun to be had,

Good company talking joking friendly,

We all started off with a cracking good walk,

Lots of talk common decency amongst,

Characters expressed humour cracking jokes,

Taking the weight off our feet on song,

Humming a cracking good tune in my head,

On a roll rolling along Irish thingamajig,

Friendly walk cracking good talk,

Scene set cracking conversation,

Discussing trials and tribulations,

Put the world to rights making alright,

Dismissing tripe cooking crackling,

All with good reason cracking season,

Obvious but not obvious just cracking,

Sums up cracking situation adds up,

Fun was had by all a good craic!

IN THE MIND

Don't need reminding own worst enemy,
It's real what I think stinks,
Trying to keep things clear for fear,
Of losing the plot all I got,
Fragile various versions on same theme,
Acted out compiling a stream,
Of ideas linking thinking,
Get together collection,
Not too jammed with space,
Juxtaposed reasonable reason,
Clear my head useless clutter,
Decide what's useful not,
Presented tempted,
All too much,
Offered deferred,
Good price trice,
Leave alone condone,
Sift through won't do,
Perception not true,
Thoughtless thoughts.

BETTER OR WORSE

Goggles put on lens inserted,
Is that better or worse?
Blurred, try this any change?
Yes, bit sharper clearer,
Right block off right eye,
Left alright, shut right,
Confused shine a light,
Can you see distant barn?
Look straight into beam,
Letter "W" follow,
Strong weak,
Up-down,
Away ground,
Different lens,
Trying all options,
Deduce by default,
Stronger weaker,
Lens shift place,
Better or worse,
Polite converse.

MAKE IT HAPPEN

To start the day with get it straight in my head,

From a list of jobs to chase up,

Obvious importance to must do,

Research possible helpers' availability,

Must phone hospital, impossible,

Left message impractical hopeful,

Have researched on a list must persist,

Self-important must wait your turn yawn,

Impatient patient persists ahead of lists,

Trying to find a way through have to,

Speak to administrator making a check,

Message left now defect differences,

Now change tack change of line,

Think of other interests to pursue,

Other interest's jobs needing assistance,

I can think of other things to do,

But singularly only my main goal rings true,

Obsessive compulsive direct main effect,

Have pushed the limits now back on transit.

PERSISTED

I had a problem with computer program,
Got advice from know-all, oh yes of course!
How many times have I got to tell you!
Reprimanded I continue abashed,
I have got to learn wrong generation,
It's simple when you know,
Paying attention now try it out,
Trying to remember what to do,
It seems all wrong but carry on,
Open two versions of the same,
Highlight text copy paste,
Yes, it's worked now save,
Now know where I am,
Sorted the problem for myself,
Confidence grows good health,
Sticky wicket good turn learnt,
Wrong then right turned out alright,
Listened to advice muddled through,
Got to keep trying don't give up!

RESILIENT

I've had a cold which has knocked the stuffing,

Out of me, lost all stamina joints weak creaking,

Knowing I'll get through this coughing spitting,

Body aching lost rhythm back out only pout,

Tripping walking difficult thinking of now,

Clear thoughts count to noughts,

Dizzy pathetic apology nonsensical,

However still thinking doable done,

Have a backlog of jobs to do stuck,

Lost my flow doing well below,

Throat sore suck tablet roll around,

Nearly choke lost swallowed,

Concentrate on deliberate,

All my time spent on survive,

Handicapped staying alive,

Drama says do or die.

Feeling immortal strive,

Hope keeps me going,

Incredible research,

Helps with my resilience.

TEMPERAMENTAL

A bit iffy unreliable changeable,

Artistic talent with variations,

Makeup ephemeral uncertain,

Far too talented for own good,

Swing in favour of then back,

Dependent correct procedure,

Keep in good books assuredly,

Definite definition lost,

Against all odds competes,

Pretentious pretence,

Vague apparition,

Hasten fortuitously,

Deferred negotiation,

Ambiguous conclusion,

For better or worse,

Assured winner loses,

Happen upon accident,

Winner takes all,

Occasion could be better.

BROKEN DOWN

Expect things to work as a matter of course,
Of course natural to think all's well,
Let down by mechanical mechanics,
Not working as they should properly,
Had been promised servicing by services,
Things go wonky over time need straightening,
Loose needs tightening by professional hand,
Parts replaced proficiently professionally,
To get back into working order provenly,
Which proves a discrepancy malfunction,
Regular servicing serves a continuum,
Stops a problem from happening first place,
Wear and tear can be tearful don't allow,
Must notice wayward discrepancy,
Professional propriety properly,
Avoids disappointment frequent,
Frequently asked questions,
Hastens smooth running smoothly,
Promiscuous profundity punctually.

REVOLVE EVOLVE

Correct etiquette of good behaviour is asked for,

Respectfully assuredly I engage with the lady on,

The line and assuredly she puts me straight,

Her domineering voice reassures me how to

continue and so I get ready to carry on with my,

Job of organising my busy life routine setting up,

And clearing away all foreseeable problems likely,

Won't hinder my progress, tittle-tattle is desugared,

Useless baggage discarded in light of

apprehended, not recommended to assist,

Narrowing down my list of prospective,

Directives that only look to hinder further,

Progress nonetheless, more help is needed,

To proceed with my prospective progression,

To unburden and nonetheless constructively,

Take further positive progressive actions,

Needed to progress further rather than go round

and around in circles

revolving not solving solutions that could concoct

progressive formula new formulations put together,

Assembled, units adjoined in such a way,

To form an evolving construction to resolve.

IT CAN WAIT

Of course it can I'll get on with other stuff,
What a patient patient patiently adapting,
Consoling the rigmarole of change,
Rearrange made interesting by contemplating,
Given me a good idea to tackle rule makers,
Officious officials need approaching head-on,
Fight fire with fire extinguish argumentative,
Trumped-up delinquents don't assist persist,
Struck off list get on with sorting all sorts,
More important solving solutions solved,
Taken time to resolve what can't wait,
At forefront top of list can't resist,
Changes how to relive highbrow,
Big thoughts come to mind of a kind,
Of retribution to retaliation getting my,
Own back for having to wait forever,
It seemed like it, time is far too precious,
A commodity to be wasted on trivial trivia,
Unproductive productions reluctant waste.

SYMPTOMATIC

———

Yes, I've got lots of symptoms if I think about it!
One comes to mind, so I act upon it,
I must straight away before it consumes,
Takes over and becomes a bigger problem,
Sensible sense orders order controller controls,
Simple and easy not taking on too much,
Within my remit remission remitted admitted,
Sensible plausible allowable allowed,
Function functional fully reasonable reasoned,
The right season for seasoning seasons,
Try to abbreviate abbreviations cut short,
The long and short of it is efficient efficiency,
My dominium is continued continuum,
Distractions causing erratic fluctuations,
Stopping my progress proficiently,
Maybe formal formality functions,
Can't possibly work under duress,
Causing me senseless derision,
Not applicable to my application.

FLEXIBLE

Must be to fit in,
Not always what I want but see,
Outside influences control decisions,
Plausible doable not incontrollable,
Dramatic change needed to rearrange,
What is necessary necessity,
What needs to happen can't happen,
Hapless hopeless nonetheless,
Confess under duress careless,
Being flexible is funny mixable,
Powerplays underway mixed up,
Out of my control bending flexible,
Over backwards pushed around,
Not happy with the sounds,
Something out of tune wrong key,
Inevitably not seen come clean,
It's happened before deploring, anymore,
Don't want to be ignored apart from,
What I'm used to apparently apparent,
Cropping up no harvest inflexible,
Directly inconceivable convinced,

Inflexible abrupt corrupt out of luck,

Hedging my chances on new perchance,

Hope to get lucky come my way,

Soon playing same old tune,

Brigadoon platoon trumpet blows,

Call of the wild elephant trumps.

LIFE IS CRAZY

As you make it, self-reflecting,
Unfortunately, a label imposed,
Only having a bit of fun, category,
It can seem crazy out of context,
A lot of life has no reason,
Fast and furious slow quickly,
Making up for lost time,
Hurry now it will soon go,
Frantic leave alone,
Panic don't want it,
How did I get into this,
How do I get out of this,
Foolishly drawn in,
In a quandary yet again.

MAKING LIGHT

Of a dark situation only have to listen to the news,

The dark side highlighted sensationalised,

The topical topics exaggerated not wanting to

Contemplate that make the news dynamic,

Misconstrued abused confused heavy,

Usually shocking shocked dark side,

Along for the ride of said contrite,

Can't abide disruptive paint it black,

Printed in the newspaper black and white,

Dogmatic taking sides political confides,

Swayed by opinion opinionated opinions,

Depending on which newspaper you read,

Feeds your mind with said kind,

Moribund deviation poor relation deviates,

As of late permeates prominently,

The lack of permeates extensions seen.

IMPROVISING

Life, making things up as I go along,
Pushed this way then that disabling,
Must settle for the mean what I mean is,
Average is best solution averaging out,
Trying my best usual conquest manifests,
Diligently diligent set repent no argument,
Enough said improve improvement,
Fully approved appropriately directly,
Disseminating regulation regularly,
Before it's too late to regulate,
Get better improve approve of,
The very thing concerning concern,
Albeit a derogatory infidelity,
Pure as driven snow,
Several degrees below,
Make ourselves warm by,
Not accepting the norm,
Confronting jurisdiction,
Belittling at large counterfeit,
Bank notes sold on sale.

RECOGNITION

Analyse what I see can it be I think it's reality,
Real or pretentious feel concealed within,
Or without the reason to believe plausible,
Unbelievable but knowing how variety differs,
From person to person an amalgamation,
Of influences experiences what been through,
All adds up to what we are changed rearranged,
The ability to adapt to different settings,
Exchanges recollections views demands,
Make us flexible bend straight delegate,
Comprehend not relate steer away from,
Acceptance or rejection deride abide,
Want to hide away from absolution,
Committed conviction correlating to,
Being a part taking part with art,
Resolving absolving resolutely,
Constructively building bridges,
To cross different beliefs ways,
Navigate a way through meanders,
Pretenders deflect deviators absolvers,
Cajole parole board afford fully paid off,
With time spent recompense never again.

I NEED HELP

As much as anything someone to talk to,
A friendly friend to understand comprehend,
It could be anybody agreeable make amends,
Don't want to overburden a conversation,
With my finicky problems a broad sweep,
Understand mine and theirs talk laugh,
Respect people's space fall from grace,
Problem shared problem solved,
Talk around issues make sense,
Get other people's opinions collaborate,
Talk and be heard upfront be heard,
Be taken in conversation snowballing,
Get on house on fire ignore denier,
Not so solitary companionship not a blip,
Power of friendship camaraderie binds,
Power of two heads together clever,
Warmth shiver moving together,
Combine remind collaborate,
Friend no hate as of late.

TECHNOLOGY BAFFLES

Sure does like a raffle,
Technician has moved from home moan,
This leaves me all at sea,
Common sense doesn't offer recompense,
Tangled up in blue what to do?
Trying my best muddy conquest,
Doing the wrong thing is blinking,
Erased confused haze,
Logically working things out,
What seems right can be wrong,
In the maelstrom conundrum,
Often must shut down pronoun,
Professional dysfunctional conventional,
Comply defy do it again know what I mean,
Frustration deregulation regulating regularly,
Got to operate systematically best options,
Avoiding malfunctions confusing issues,
Disruptive disposition disposes abruptly.

THINK FOR MYSELF

Big boy now doesn't need help,
Happy with my settings surroundings,
Secure able to work produce,
Keep it simple within reach,
Get myself organised ready,
For anything anytime,
Presentable presence of mind,
Setup level start suitable job,
Depending on correct incentive,
Thinking how to proceed,
Things to do what's needed?
Stop thinking of myself,
Others need help,
Must concede give up greed,
Adapt to always taking,
Generous partaking,
Defect reflect connect,
Thoughtlessness stubborn,
Automatic doing,
Change resolve,
Can be generous,

Towards most,
Don't think of cost,
Altruistic effective,
Good subjective,
Connect reflective,
Deflect demands,
Singular objective,
Making doing,
All enjoying,
Pleasure reciprocated,
Back on myself,
For giving up wealth,
Of ideas commandeered,
Knowledge is free,
Experience tells,
Give up sales talk,
Go for walk,
Over and beyond,
Friendly correspond,
A helping hand,
Expands friends,
When make amends,
Comprehend.

FAIR PLAY

Fair enough good fare for lunch,

Fairly ambitious frivolous frivolity,

Fractious functionality formally,

Coming to fruition forthwith,

Without any formal appraisal,

Applied by the applicant aforesaid,

Conductively conducting conduct,

With paramount importance,

Impetuously per say,

Improper petulance,

Discovered by,

Per petulantly aforesaid,

With hindsight kicks ass,

Expert experience expertly,

Exponentially straight ahead,

A transition translated barbarically,

Allows for all discrepancies,

Furthermore, without delay,

Apparent promiscuous habits,

Letting the side down unfairly.

WINTER STORMS

One after another names prevail,
Trees and debris blown down around,
Flooding building damage stay in,
Personal damage nothing new,
Sun breaks through still in charge,
Shine on my conundrum,
Always waiting next involve,
Lazy comply,
Feel dull dizzy,
Confused vacant,
Engaged taken,
To make happen,
Up to me responsibility,
It will blow over,
Wind down,
Back to normal,
Change subliminal,
From within without,
No authority doubt,
Soul destroyed blown away,
Nevertheless,
Humbled.

NAMBI-NAMBI

A new term come from politics,

I must interpret, not really up to the job,

In this context hasn't got full support from member,

A weak bill that can be easily overturned,

Probably comes from Nambi-Pambi,

Childish behaviour not assertive,

This reckoning does sum up the situation,

Dead reckoning a positive guess of where we are,

Calculated by means of plotting,

Evaluating surmounting sure thing probably,

Can't be anywhere else I'm positive,

The fact that they're not completely sure,

Is a bit Nambi-Nambi all said and done,

Now waiting for the outcome hopeful,

To get enough support from members,

To be able to carry through become law,

Diplomatic bureaucratic both sides,

Listened to assessed Nambi-Nambi.

WATER

I've just been swimming fully immersed,
In this solid liquid surface tension holding,
This entity mercury fluid melds together,
Submerged held buoyant pushing along,
Body strength surges through paddle push,
Arms draw legs kick flip swimming motion,
Pull through dive surface splash crash,
Digging rolling stretching out holding,
Breathing bubbling expiring maintaining,
Rhythm pattern order solutions solution,
Left-right arms legs propel buoyancy,
Maintained arms push out up along,
Twist turn follow lane look out watch,
Reach breaststroke assertively asserts,
Avoid dark mass under water as seen,
Body puddle duck avoid own way,
Harmless harassed hearsay controversy,
Flappy arms backstroke consumes whole lane,
Call attendant for chairlift up away dare say,
All done routine complied with efficiently.

CELEBRATE RESOLVING

Is something I must do more often,
A pat on the back self-confidence,
Sometimes I do as a matter of course,
Without realising its importance,
Then on reflection well done!
It could be an issue if left,
Assessing what's been done,
Lifts the weight carrying,
Had to decide to confide,
Ask for advice talk through,
Don't know it all know all,
Anxiety lifted by changing,
Order of play delayed,
Wait my turn I've learnt,
Hold back from flak,
Is a good crack,
Do unto others as yourself,
Common decency fraternity,
Resolved happily,
Feel-good factor matters.

SYSTEMIC

There are always ways to comply with,

Officious officials offering complicating,

Abiding taking part in certain complications,

The order to comply law-abiding don't defy,

Morally correct defect seamlessly seeming,

Not dreaming contravening deliberate leaning,

Following the line path route laid out corridor,

Travelled along until the correct door is found,

Branching out openings open into,

A better state of mind a clearer view of new,

Detecting plausible acceptable rings true,

Method to my madness fully applicable applies,

Don't deride it makes me happy to follow,

A route systematic sustainable obligatory,

Conforming to said rules of the game plan,

In picture frame clear view of what to do,

Simple conforming to reasonable,

Assumptions assuming for the duration,

A systemic outlook of compatibility,

Complying with a simplistic formulation,

For the duration navigating through all,

Corridors of power plays towering above,

Looking down on ascending comprehensions,

That I don't fully understand comprehend,

Driving me around the bend apprehend?

TRYING TOO HARD

———

It can happen without realising,

I was pushing the river instead of letting it flow,

Being held back by the undertow,

Bringing me down, wanting to be up,

Losing a grip, fraught not relaxed,

Wanting something too much,

But out of touch with myself,

Thought I needed progression advance,

But was being tripped over jumping fence,

Hold back not too fast solutions last,

Recall what's been done before.

Find that place mood proceeds,

Get it back absorb hold on,

To past recollections success,

That order of play delivering,

It will happen so let it, stand back,

Easy does, problem solved,

Forget its importance then,

Room is allowed for development.

HOW I'VE CHANGED

From how I used to be,

I'm aware of a gradual change called growing up,

Accepting differences opinions attitudes,

Softened hardened rejected thoughts collected,

More thoughtful easy-going flexible,

Dogmatic dog left behind barking mad,

Sensible sense now commenced,

Recommended collected gathered,

Hindsight wise old man forward looking,

Come to booking no foul play!

Don't mind bit of controversy,

Still outspoken feel forsaken,

Haven't always got it right blight,

Left humbled grumbled,

Contentious not annulled,

Consciously consoled,

Not always delivered,

Keeping myself to myself,

In terms of wealth stealth,

Appreciate company,

Rather than alone,
Friendly on telephone,
Not too abrupt when see sense.

89

CHANGING LAYOUT

To make things fit I've had to reorganise,
Shuffle the pack deal new hand,
Everything's got its place in place,
Try to ergonomically fit more,
Surely there is room for everything,
Haven't done it this way before,
Try it out see if it works,
Soon know if it doesn't,
Tripping over can't remember,
New is supposed to bring on change,
Rearrange plane plain,
Different not the same,
Navigate away from hearsay,
Others' opinions not realistic,
Don't have to live with it,
What seemed a good idea,
Wasn't Ikea flat pack,
Put together followed,
Instructions to the letter,
Orderly order ordered.

ABSTRACT DESCRIPTION

———

Abstract description more of a revelation of,

How things appear to be, trying to make sense,

Of day-to-day living politely convening replying,

Being a part of started previously importantly,

Must have been to have got this far in surely,

Trying to improve make things better,

In life's charade of cut-and-paste haste,

Quickly now time is money made work to be done,

Got the contract now deadline towards working,

With haste contractors confident get done,

Cut through when there's more to do can do,

Must trust in others confidence to comply,

Professional application finishing off the,

Said contract dutifully well on time not,

Having to be reminded application assertively,

Completed up to standard expected without,

Being corrected or penalizing unexpected,

Proper job done as laid down contract completed.

Not going to be defeated revenue deserved,

In a word abstract deserves definition,

Bearing no correlation abstract comprehension.

ABSTRACT THOUGHTS

Have a purpose for me,
Able to explore different avenues,
Not restricted by anything,
Having to conform morally,
The door is now open unrestricted,
Which means I can think freely,
Anything goes got the freedom,
Not representing copying photographing,
Questioning how to think broadly openly,
Engaging rearranging new format,
Levelled dishevelled combinations,
Combining refining defining differences,
Subjective objective collective,
Communicating aesthetic arbitration,
Like it or not it's what we got,
Similar dissimilar important trivial,
All for and against provocative,
Diligent rule breaker discriminates,
Level-headed anarchist against.

DEALING DAILY

With the usual kafuffle spells trouble,
Having to sort out problems made for myself,
Casually getting in too deep innocently,
Trouble laid before me should know better,
Life is full of trickery daylight robbery,
This happens far too easily matter of course,
I shouldn't have to keep checking legal,
Assertiveness correctness jumping hurdles,
Avoiding tripping over own feet delete,
Competition competes keep neat,
Safely saving coordinating ordering,
Correct defect deficient left out,
More to constructing building,
Revealing structure to manufacture,
Easy from kit form put together adorn,
Assembled resembled concocted,
New delivery assertive assertively,
Common practice practically,
Dealt with subliminally in turn,
Shuffle the pack deal reveals.

MEANT

What I meant was I think you've misunderstood,
Me, I thought I had made it clear that I'm trying,
My best to be honest straight meaning relate,
Communicate exchange ideas do not complicate,
Don't muddy the waters I'm standing in please,
By all means, offer criticism constructively,
Good or bad happy sad Jack the lad,
Apologetic pathetic reason pleasing,
Meaning trying my best in life's conquest,
To vilify not deny different ways to approach,
A whole new gambit of ideas solutions,
Meaningfully resolutely solving,
The aforesaid problematic dysfunctional,
Critical acclaim claiming to be the be-all,
And end-all of further disruption not,
Hitherto forth pronunciations,
That when hurled at an objector,
Sound in a despicable manner,
Meant for discouragement,
To those that can't relent,
Know what I mean meant,
Causing an argument.

EVERYTHING DIFFICULT

It seems to be confusing trivial,
People don't understand and make things worse,
I must be alert to complications,
Difficulties persist unresolved list,
Taken too much on can't resist,
Keep it simple refuse must do,
Have to can do stupid not to,
Want to love to maybe do,
Too many options to take,
Leave alone tricky dicky,
Implicit demands assert,
Offers offered to suit,
Themselves offering,
As little bargaining,
Bank borrowing avoided,
Within means by all means,
Expensive expense,
Takes my recompense,
Delivering nonsense.

NEEDING SPACE

We have booked a holiday away,
Just thinking about it expands my mind,
Watched a video layout of pools views,
Had the right effect uplifted the depressed,
Sullen sunken abandoned ship now afloat,
The capsized derided unfounded found,
Ready to play the part try on new can do,
Exotic erotic suncream glean screen scene,
Evolving away from stay-at-home stop,
Pack up put up getting in the groove,
My record had got stuck repetitive tune,
Thoughtful resolution imbued rings true,
Get ready a lot to do finish resolve,
Got to get my head around new profound,
Consider considerate left behind,
Have made allowances forgive allowed,
Each to their own safe and sound,
Space has been found share new ground.

SHOWING CHARACTER

Happens without thinking about it,
Against all odds not giving up,
Seeing the job through until complete,
Persistent resistant putting up with,
Unexpected not deflected away stay,
Stubborn stick until job done,
Solving problems answering answers,
Helping helpless to find their way,
Finding goodness from within,
Not material bound other ways,
Strength of character non detractor,
Fighting for right thing as seen,
Taking time to console unfortunates,
Not thinking solely for themselves,
Delve deeper than others would,
Endlessly out of their way to say,
Stand up for less privileged,
Decent decency projected,
Taking action not neglected.

GET CRITICISM

Yes, I get it does affect me absolutely,

Whether being misunderstood or for the good,

Or bad ignorance has its place in the race,

No disgrace it's commonplace actually,

I must listen digest accept draw on,

All part of life's conundrum,

I can feel hurt from simple remarks,

So have to quickly defend,

Make amends quip back quickly,

Smart retort levels field,

From which I can yield,

Obstinate view how seen,

Don't want must change,

Listened to extremes,

Pitch somewhere in between,

Cajole their prison sentence,

Augment accept relent argument,

Repent only if true,

Can be seen as tic-Ardy-boo,

Point taken pitch elsewhere only fair,

Considerable consideration considered,

If only they would tolerate my word,

Not always right little contrite,

I've heard defend my way,

Try to change rearrange,

Accept theirs isn't absolutely,

Mine is defiant politely!

WHAT?

Should I be doing,
Endless possibilities too much choice,
Has sent me into a tailspin of opportunities,
Thinking through of what to do project blue,
Don't know which way to turn yearn,
Nothing's chiming charming spurn,
Quizzical physical cycle it off,
Still confused used bemused,
Question what for why applies,
Often derives contrived concern,
Feeling blue nothing true,
Don't know what to do,
Making notes anecdotes,
Supress suspicion,
No correlation fitting,
Imagination trying,
Had lots to do don't want to,
Fussy pointless confess,
Duress countless reasons.

WONDERFUL
WARWICKSHIRE TWO

I went for a little drive through villages,
That opened into rural countryside,
Proudly converted ram shackled,
Barns austere facades done up,
Cheaply common as muck development,
Barns paddocks at rear dogs' bark,
Horses represent affordable status,
All on show to be admired,
Polished off the hoof brassy,
Gymkhana representing,
Horse boxes play away,
Rosette winners trained,
White ribbon down to hoof,
Hoof hearted regiment,
Pony club friends adhere,
Out and about trot on,
Emblazoned balustrade,
Status symbol repeated,
All over the county,
Fastidious ugly brazen,

South fork cowboy,

J. Rs 4x4 Sue Ellen,

Bit rich tidy bitch,

Gymkhana shows,

Lads play rugger,

Rugby school,

Privately educated.

SETTING UP

All part of organising ready to start,
Clearing the decks making room,
Setting straight things in the way,
Can now move forward unhindered,
Discarded clutter recycled reused,
Whatever's new has second life,
Efficient commodity a lottery,
What's new must be thought of,
What to do when old sold,
All things considered how to get rid of,
A beginning and an end depend,
On life expectancy born again,
Priced in conforming out clause,
Pushes price up expensive,
Commodity looks cheap,
More to evaluation all considered,
Reconstituted not polluted,
Thought and design combine,
Life expectancy more to it,
Old and new rebuild setup.

PARADOX

Of life I'm only happy when I'm unhappy!

Call me a headbanger stupid boy idiot,

But there's something in it up against,

A contrary flighty fairy fairly compares me,

To just like so-and-so above below,

Knows doesn't know seamlessly seeming,

Beaming sad glad mad friendly angry,

All emotions causing commotion in control,

Out of the ordinary common decency dismissed,

Contemplating navigating away from trouble,

Which arrives as a matter of course just,

Life's happenings demanding attention,

Interesting gains my way wanting to play,

Needless necessity endless conformity,

Drawing singularity out of implausible,

Crop up without realising just happening,

Grabbing my attention away from intentions,

Accidental interesting incidents turn my attention,

Into a better forthcoming fortuitous advantageous,

Event unexpectedly profiteering profit gain,

Turning around absolution absolutely,
Unequitable without a doubt amounting,
To nothing gained nothing lost costs.

105

PERSONAL SUBJECTIVE

Cycling along country road,
Birds are used to me, singing warning tune,
I reply imitate best that I can,
They reiterate warning,
Beautiful louder rasping through,
Automatic threat territory invaded,
I pass by accept, warned off,
I think my retort is fair replication,
Probably insolent invasion,
Privacy entered abashed,
Deflected quashed deferred,
Raucous magpie swoops threat,
My insolence not accepted,
Fought off rejected,
Silly birds oh my words!
Affected disturbed,
Beauty appreciated,
Space accident navigated,
Around respect their sound,
Personally mitigated,
Love belated consecrated.

SUBTITLES

"He laughs out loud" and "the crowd cheers!"

"There is an overwhelming sense of happiness,"

"The camera pans across fraternity,"

"A joyous scene, an act of chivalry,"

"Music quieter, people embrace each other,"

Scene is set, "For convivial promiscuity!"

"Drink and be merry," "logs thrown on the fire,"

"Companionship to the heart's desire,"

"The fire roars, adding to happy atmosphere,"

"Party people mingle," "embracing the evening,"

All that's needed is "Mince pies and port,"

"Drink to your health and much wealth!"

"A seasoned actor" non detractor,

"Raising glasses and atmosphere forth with,"

A commander commandeering, "golden earring!"

"Pleasing partaking punctual presence promptly!"

Describing each act with promiscuity prevalently,

"Bumptious scrummage prevails off rails!"

IT WILL ALL COME CLEAR

No fear my dears, clouds will disappear,

Revealing a natural way forward,

Given time what needs to be done,

Will become obvious planning,

Order of play will say what's next,

Indivisible at first intuition concurs,

Didn't think it was possible now reasonable,

This seems to fit born of habit habitual,

Proceeding by leading role in charge,

Full control responsible ordering,

Surprised myself friendly stealth,

Hidden charm out of the blue,

Conscripting friends' full amends,

Show how I've changed rearranged,

Offering goodwill what I'll do is,

Resolve involves trust people I don't know,

To fix the job stand over to see clearly,

That it's done up to scratch convincingly,

Clearly indiscriminately reliably asserted.

GOING WELL

Things look up promising clear,
No fear not worried assured certain,
Convivial liveable doable done,
Likeable love it's lovely truly,
Spring just around the corner,
Snowdrops daffodils showing,
Milder air spring in my stride,
Confident not taken for ride,
Simplistic ordinary naturally,
Going with the flow above below,
Conciliatory conformation no,
Regulation from delegation,
Deregulated positive output,
Constructive productive,
Producing products aplenty,
Heaven sent me conformity,
Duality singularity dumbfounded,
Of course, right course accepted,
John Lennon sings good tune in tune.

STICK TO YOUR GUNS!

You must be self-assured not put off,
Life is so variable changeable anytime,
Set out your goals aims don't deflect,
Keep on keeping-on persistence,
Reliable will show through assuredly,
Consistent persistent not going to give up,
If I stick around surely safe and sound,
Gaining ground profoundly stubbornly,
Safe bet pair of hands my command,
Not going to pretend commend,
Know where I am convincing,
Morally correct not going to defect,
Problem shared problem solved,
Solid functional not dysfunctional,
Want to be seen as reliable always,
Assertive is my directive,
Positive affirmative simply surely,
A matter of fact known direct,
Boring sharing comparing compare.

TEMPTING SUN

It's drawing me out away from my work,
Disregarding what I should be doing,
Beating down making me feel good,
Absorbing the rays suncream on,
Looking back at my workstation,
Now poor relation no invitation,
The temptress is winning playing away,
Back and forth catch moment,
Cloud covers straight back in,
Sun losing soon passes,
Back to praising thinking,
Working planning two things,
At once absorbing returning,
At station yearning drawing,
Away paying homage losing,
Back to absorbing rays' daze,
The temptress won't discuss,
High order of importance,
Attend to must do ought to,
This then that making a prat.

I KNOW EXACTLY WHERE IT IS

So please let it be and leave alone,

I know where to find it,

Where I last left it, it's now home,

To my travel bag spare space taken,

It loiters and hangs out there,

I'm comfortable with it,

If I moved it wouldn't know where to put it,

I'm happy it's happy everybody's happy,

Perhaps it could be rehoused somewhere else,

I'm going to have to think long and hard,

There must be a solution to finding room,

It would be better in a cupboard if cleared,

Away under the coats and jackets to live,

I'll have to remember where I've put it,

I'll assign a new inventory invented,

Comprehended understood I would,

It would be much tidier not gathering dust,

I must for wanderlust get accomplished,

A bit of a find to remind of a kind positively.

CLIMATE CHANGE

Getting used to waves of extremes as ordinary,
Blocks of weather getting stuck a kink,
In the jet stream persistent resistant,
Weather can now be predicted in streams,
Phases of wet then dry foreseen,
Wet season tropical low then high,
Predictions of all or nothing comply,
Warm staying warm but wet season,
High pressure gets stuck kink season,
Warm sunny hot can't be budged,
Upper hemisphere staying clear,
Now in for extremes get used to,
Windy gales prevail over again,
Flooding without warning dawning,
Can't predict interim persists promptly,
Erratic dramatic occurrence prevails,
No end to inconsistency irreversible,
Must now put up with unpredictable,
In for trouble unactable double trouble.

BLOCK

Sometimes my mind goes blank,
Can't think what to do have got stuck,
It might be writer's block no way to turn,
I'm looking for something waiting,
I suppose I've got to make it happen,
It's up to me to get inventive organise,
Move problems out of the way unblock,
First must realise what the problem is,
Seeing the restriction malfunction,
Get my mojo working.
What has relieved is respected,
Other people's good work subjected,
See how I can help with reciprocation,
I must now follow in return with a,
Good commendation reviews true blue,
Only fair to respond with good compare,
They have eased the way I must with,
All decency respond correctly well done!
Now feel like a block party invite everybody.

FOYER

Come and go,

Café time busy,

Card beeper opens,

Doors through,

Pastel-coloured chairs,

Striding out,

Back and forth,

Café time meet,

Cups carried back,

Nurse's uniform,

Space divides,

Purpose office,

Important job,

Professional stance,

Invisible romance,

Half chance,

Caught glance,

Happening place,

Through and through.

CHOICE OF WORDS

I must choose carefully for fear of saying the,
Wrong thing being misunderstood,
It's easy to get it wrong come across as blunt,
Tactless cause crude rude misconstrued,
Taken the wrong way alternative delivery,
Pronunciation can literally confuse issues,
Sounds wrong got it wrong not clear,
Also, double meanings same but different,
Spring water, spring tide, spring to your feet,
Sprinkle, sprinkled, sprinkler, spring season,
Springer, coiled spring, spring sprung, springs,
Bed springs, spring in your stride, spring bank
Holiday, spring in your shoes, springtime,
Watch spring, spring greens, spring flowers,
Springtime of the year, springy deflection,
Springboard, spring off the tongue, spring,
Daffodils, step into spring, spring bounce,
Spring it to you, spring off one another,
Spring it on you, clock spring, car springs.

LIFE DRAWING

From a pose naked lady charcoal to paper,
I haven't done for fifty years since art college,
I have practiced still-life drawing to keep my hand,
In now not shaking relish the challenge,
Have got a decent-sized drawing pad,
Sticks of charcoal ready to let go,
I remember my art teacher showing me,
How to set out sections head to feet,
Then work quickly not getting stuck,
On details, sketch freely shapely,
Getting curves swerves arms legs,
Into place don't worry about face,
There's no disgrace body beautiful,
Get the essence down draw around,
Character captured making pronounced,
Working around the figure adding,
Lines charcoal is forgiving can be smudged,
Away drawn over corrected easily,
Got the figure represented carefully,
The essence of depiction characterfully,
Showing personality traits relate,

Seem to have done enough not,
Overworked fully presentable,
Represented drawn down.

FIT INTO PLACE

Good when things do without trouble,

I believe you make your own luck,

By correctly positioning and connecting,

Allowing presentation representation,

Showing respect to order of play,

To be taken seriously honestly,

It all comes back on delivery presentation,

People expect decent delivery,

All four give me five staying alive,

Not two contrived adds up to sixes,

And sevens get digital eight nine,

Combine refined ten, legs eleven,

Twelve delve, unlucky thirteen,

Fourteen goes in-between fifteen,

Sixteen, seventeen belated eighteen,

Nineteen to the top twenty is plenty,

Twenty-one free birthday boy party,

Reckless senseless what to do?

Twenty-two I ask you can do,

Twenty-three next commodities,

Twenty-four don't bore,

Twenty-five always strive,

Haphazard twenty-six,

Depicts conflicts war,

Unstable twenty-seven,

Driven twenty-eight as of late,

Confiscate twenty-nine all mine,

Thirty hurt me, thirty-one aplomb,

Thirty-two innocents do,

Thirty-three can it be?

Plagiarize thirty-four copies,

Want some more,

Done for thirty-five,

Picking up flicks thirty-six,

Thirty-seven driven,

Thirty-eight complicate,

Thirty-nine combines,

With forty to make one,

Onto forty-two,

Raptures forty-three,

Cannibalize forty-four,

Do it some more forty-five,

Habitual forty-six,

Avoid conflict forty-seven,

Forty-eight shut gates,
Smell permeates forty-nine,
Fresh air fifty,
Drives away fifty-one,
Change mind fifty-two,
Fifty-three can't be,
Fifty-four all for,
Fifty-five still alive,
Fifty-six pick up sticks,
Fifty-seven gone,
Fifty-eight as of late,
Permeate fifty-nine,
Sixty does it,
Sixty-one albums,
Sixty-two true blues,
Efficient sixty-three,
Sixty-four candours,
Sixty-five still alive,
Sixty-six pensioners,
Old still fitting into place.

TAKEN

Borrowed, stolen, had, will return, a given,
Theft nicked pinched scrumped temper relieved,
Temporary exemption promises to return,
Unlawful retention of deeds objects,
Without permission deliberate detention,
Captured kidnapped imprisoned retained,
Held passed over buried not seen liberty,
Conscience not clear robbed of sobriety,
Defunct useless had its day lost soul,
No pride broken down out of time dead,
Got over collection prized possession,
Harboured relinquished forthwith said,
Abashed commitment foiled tarnished,
The gloss off dull barely seen blind,
Improper conduct arbitration vague,
All sense and sensibility impoverished,
Right of way blocked fenced off keep out,
My rights dishevelled improper determination.

DREARY DAY

———

That's to say grey still nothing happening,

My mood reflects this nothingness,

Flat compact dull waiting for something,

Don't know what, it's so quiet,

Someone speak break bleak,

I need company to accompany,

Avoiding trash radio talk music,

That won't relieve my sinking,

Ship water coming in around,

Up to my knees drowning,

Waiting for rescue boat,

To help me float,

Back up rise above,

Surface tension breaking,

Through muddle,

Brittle snap,

Thinking back,

Memory shift,

Better times remind,

All-seeing eyes,

Dreariness away,

Decent decency,
Practical practice,
Need accomplice.

124

I'LL GET BACK TO YOU

Just getting started is an ordeal too much,
Checking messages apparent pledges,
Confessing, more or lessing demanding,
Apprehending unknown condescending,
Want to get on with thought consideration,
I've got my own plans desires contrivers,
Fighting through misconstrued follow through,
A lot to do want to can't do probably should,
Being held back by overzealous apparitions,
Got to keep it simple steps in line confine,
Pushing too hard gets baffled blinded,
Then when I've sieved through what to do,
Difficulties disappear construction reappears,
With no fear of repetition dereliction confuse,
Dismissing all to abundant redundant ideas,
Set back in arrears left behind only to remind,
Of unfortunate adventures promiscuous,
Proposals present problems irreversible,
So, I promise to get back to your didgeridoo,
That will do, confirm said to do.

THIS DYSTOPIAN HELL

———

Side of life to shock,
When I watch news on TV,
They show the worst get attention.
"You might find,
Some of these scenes upsetting!"
Attention sought "can't look away!"
Gruesome disturbing realism,
Taken to the front line!
Everything visible by video,
Soldiers interviewed at the front,
Action-packed "Actively Active."
It is shocking death bombing,
We all know better,
Stop deadly competitor!
Taking sides derides,
All the same but different,
Simplistic relent,
Stops the argument,
Patronise the bigot,
Causing the upset.

NO GOING BACK

Forward is the only way of delivery,
Improvements of efficiency can be made,
To help improve orderly transition change,
Rearrange contents offer new display,
Comparable differences deferred displayed,
Change of inventory reinvented recalculated,
The not-so-bad sense of sensibility lifts,
My outlook showing bright horizons,
Not thinking of going too far but far enough,
To say I've been away change hither say,
Accommodating different scenes of obscurity,
To reset my mind friend's opinions not before,
I've studied a map. Not going back transition,
Flack adventurous mischievous excitedly,
Explore unusual haven't been here before,
Want to see more of the same new picture frame,
Kind of marching on new appraisal singsong,
Taking new breath of fresh air au contraire,
All tributaries leading me to the sea romantically,
Stirred up a soul of enjoyment new enrolment,
To the good life leaving behind strife.

STAND YOUR GROUND

So much of life is ephemeral you must assert,
Things change positions become vacant,
Must reassess to enter same old game,
Reassure enter passwords reconfigure,
The master copy default gets copied,
The wide web world interlinked helping,
Thieving taking making must be with it to,
Play along get to work with messaging,
Communicate get with it or lose out,
It's always busy frantic don't panic!
Get people to help know where to ask,
Follow set path avoid risky business,
Dead certainty truly confidently plausibly,
Stand up to people wanting to infringe,
Put the phone down on sulfureous brown,
Don't offer personal details sending off rails,
Avoid catchy catch there to catch out,
Catch-22 promises to imbue ring true,
Personality must be assessed forget rest,
Life's conquest always put to test invest.

FEELING BETTER

At last shaken off lingering cold,
That's been with me uninvited persistently,
I stood up back straight deep breath,
Head felt clear ready for far and near,
Want to take on commandeer,
I will tread correctly gingerly,
Carefully organise purposefully,
Put into place start the race,
Held back by rain waiting for plain,
Seems to be fine persistent on last,
Raincheck that will drive through,
Sure to look out Peter storm,
Ready for English weather whatever,
Now not under the weather all considered,
Fully prepared want to dare compare,
Brave face meets the race head on,
Only bit of rain don't complain,
Soon dry off after had enough,
Contrary country, blighty alrighty,
Brought up to accept good camping weather,
Whatever the weather with or without,
Certainly, talk about it hope for better.

SIGNS OF FATIGUE

Tiredness making wrong decisions,
Says it's time to step back from the front line,
Digging a hole going deeper in swallowing,
Staying on the edge lonesome pledge,
Too much of anything is an addiction,
Abstemious keeping out of repetitive shout,
Alarm bells should ring overdone thing,
Delicate procedure of living song singing,
Making decisions thoughtful renditions,
Policy kept effect's ability to deflect,
Shrug off unwanted pressures demands,
Carrying the weight of delivery unsurmountable,
Double pressure reasserted not averted,
Living up to expectations poor relations,
Can't be avoided trouble annoyed with,
Tiredness takes its toll apology annulled.

ALLOWANCES MADE

Although I have Multiple Sclerosis MS,
I try to lead as normal a life as possible,
I have acquired devices to overcome deficiencies,
With these aids I can hide foot drop tripping,
Glasses to cover faulty vision eye blank,
Rollator to walk around house,
Trike to cycle along road,
Wheelchair when can't,
Chair lift upstairs,
Economically designed,
Must be driven,
Taxi handy,
Carer cares for me,
Takes me swimming,
Disabled toilets,
Access through doors,
Wider seats,
All common practice,
Made perfect.

ABOUT ATMOSPHERE PRESS

Founded in 2015, Atmosphere Press was built on the principles of Honesty, Transparency, Professionalism, Kindness, and Making Your Book Awesome. As an ethical and author-friendly hybrid press, we stay true to that founding mission today.

If you're a reader, enter our giveaway for a free book here:

SCAN TO ENTER
BOOK GIVEAWAY

If you're a writer, submit your manuscript for consideration here:

SCAN TO SUBMIT
MANUSCRIPT

And always feel free to visit Atmosphere Press and our authors online at atmospherepress.com. See you there soon!

ABOUT THE AUTHOR

Anthony P Prior

Please let me introduce myself.

I am sixty-six retired writing full time!

Trained as an artist BA. Bristol 79,

Furthered myself diploma psychology,

James Joyce summer school,

Writing is fun suits my lifestyle,

I am disabled with MS can do hence large text,

I live with my wife supporting each other,

Active mind helps me remind,

Two lads now adults granddad,

I have pursued self-publishing with,

Publishing Push producing two books,

Stream of Consciousness,

Actively Active, both KDP Kindle eBooks,

I am a self-made person self-employed,

Ran own boatbuilding business,

Built my own house.